CHILDREN'S FASHION
ILLUSTRATION

グラフィック社

CHILDREN'S FASHION ILLUSTRATION

by Kojiro Kumagai ©

Copyright © 1990 by Graphic-sha Publishing Co., Ltd.
1-9-12, Kudan-kita, Chiyoda-ku Tokyo 102 Japan

ISBN4-7661-0579-6

First published in December 25th 1990

Translation by Joseph W. Walker and Kiyoko Walker, color
analyst.

Printed in Japan by Kinmei Printing Co., Ltd.

はじめに

"ファッションイラストレーションの描き方" もレディース, メンズと続き, 本書は「子どもの描き方」となりました。
このファッションイラストレーションのシリーズは, イラストレーター, ファッションデザイナーの方々には, 基礎として, どうしても欠かすことのできないものです。

イラストレーションや絵画の世界でも, すばらしい作品というものは, 少なくとも基礎の上に成り立っているものです。基礎がしっかりできなければ, 応用もアイデアも, よいものは出来ません。

　本書の子どもの描き方は, イラストレーター, ファッションデザイナーを目指している人達のために, 子どものプロポーションから顔の描き方, 洋服の部分練習, 着装の仕方などを, 誰にでも解りやすく, 簡単に描けるように解説してあります。
さらに, 色の塗り方や素材の描き方を, テキストとして役立つように編集しました。
さあ, この本を手にしたら, すぐに勉強をしてみましょう。

Prologue

How to draw children is the third in a series of fashion illustration books. It follows books on illustrating men's and women's fashion by the same author. This series is indispensable as a basic study guide for future fashion designers and illustrators.

In the field of art and illustration excellent work stands firmly on a foundation of basic study. Without experience in the basics, no matter how good your ideas are, you can not apply them to wider use.

This book is to enable those who wish to be fashion designers or illustrators to easily draw the faces, figures and clothes of children in correct proportion.

It also covers the ways to draw and color various fabrics. It has many detailed study exercises, so it is useful as a textbook.

So, as soon as you get this book, begin studying.

目 次
Contents

顔の描き方（プロポーション）
How to draw faces (Proportions)

3才 Three years old　　　5才 Five years old　　　7才 Seven years old

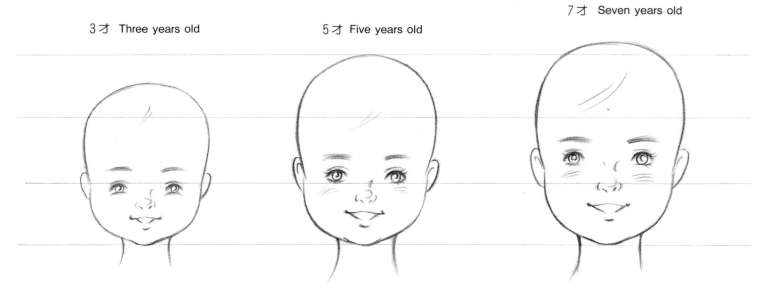

正面向き　Front view

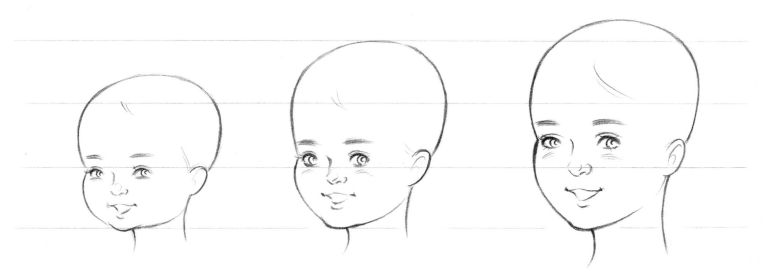

斜め向き　Oblique profile

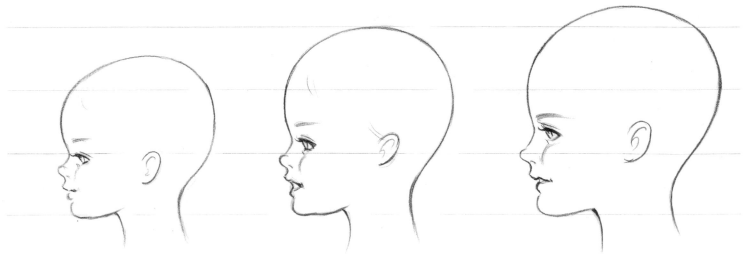

横向き　Profile

10才 Ten years old　　　17才 Seventeen years old

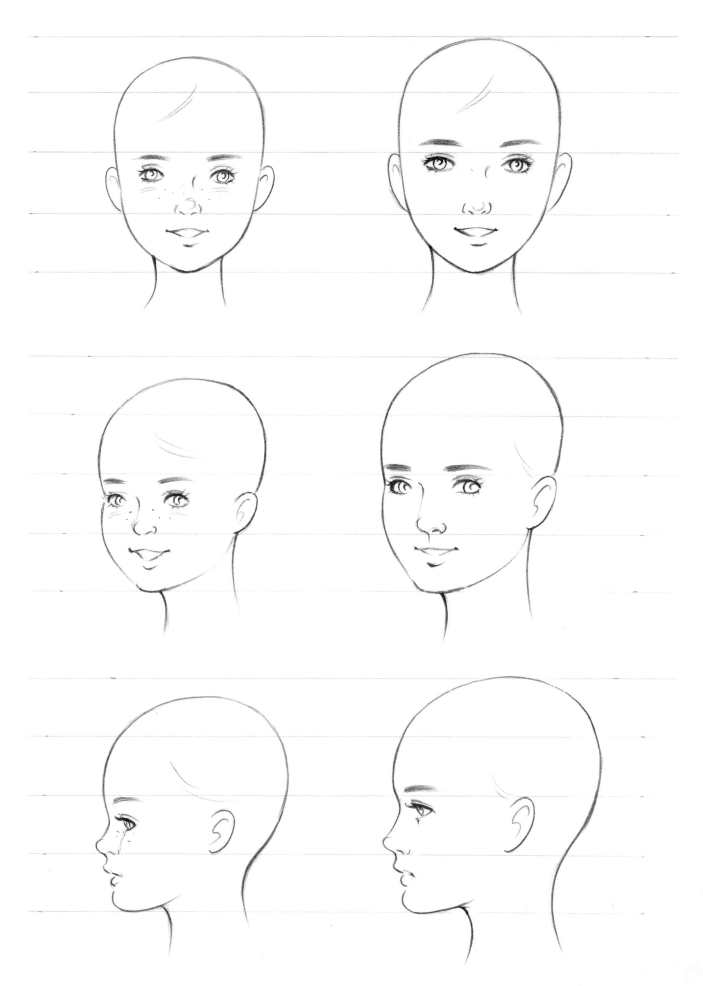

顔&ヘアの描き方

How to draw faces and hair

3才　Three years old

5才　Five years old

7才　Seven years old

正面向き　Front view

斜め向き　Oblique profile

横向き　Profile

10才　Ten years old　　　　　　　　　17才　Seventeen years old

顔の描き方応用 Study exercises for drawing faces

0才から3才 From infants to age three

プロポーションの描き方

子どものプロポーションは，成長の段階に応じて変化が著しく，年令によってバランスが違います。赤ちゃんのように年令が低いほど，全体から見て頭の割合が大きく，成長するにしたがって，その割合が小さくなります。

年令が低いほど，細く短い首，やゝ小さな肩，突きでたお腹が特徴で，手や足はふっくらと丸く描きましょう。

How to draw proportions

Children's proportions change extremely from one stage of growth to the next. They have a different balance according to their age. The younger they are, the larger their heads are, and the closer their proportions are to that of infants. As they grow older their heads become proportionally smaller. The younger they are, the slimmer and shorter their necks are with rather small shoulders, projecting stomachs and plump, round arms and legs. Draw them in this way.

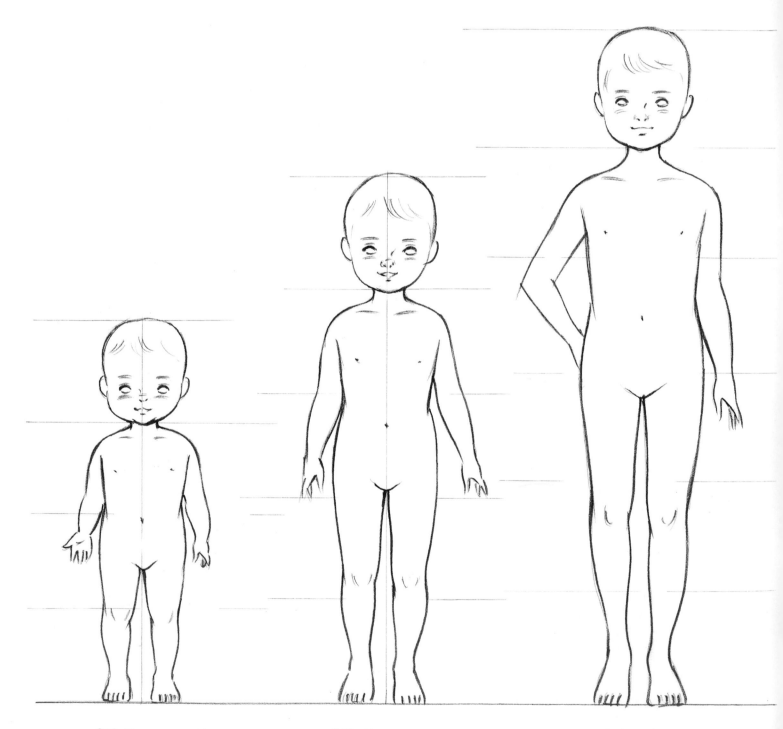

3才　Three years old   5才　Five years old   7才　Seven years old

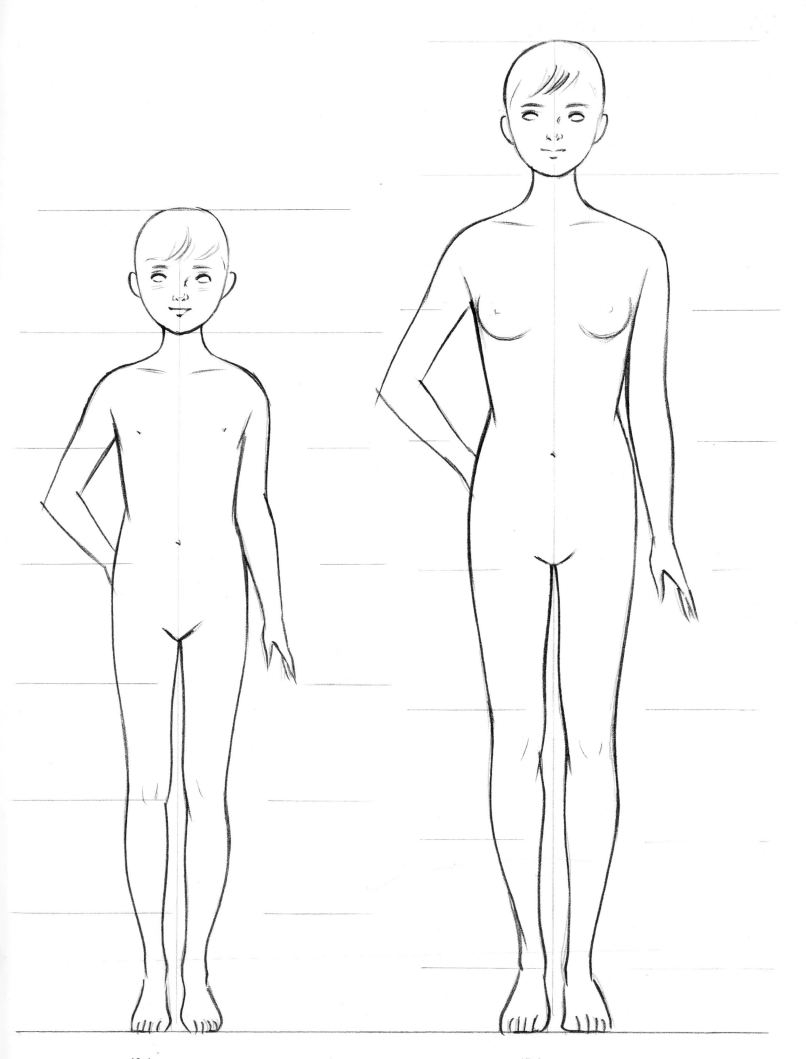

12才　Twelve years old

17才　Seventeen years old

着装

着装で大切なことは，洋服のシルエットと着た時に，身体にフィットするところと，身体から離れているところがどこなのかを知ることです。
身体の動きによっても違ってきますので，自分が鏡の前で研究することも大事なことです。

Clothing

The important things to consider in drawing clothing are the silhouette and those parts of the costume which fit to the body or are loose on the body. Because these change according to movement of proportions, it is important to study them closely in front of a mirror.

3才　Three years old

5才　Five years old

7才　Seven years old

12才　Twelve years old

17才　Seventeen years old

プロポーションの描き方応用
●３才から５才

頭が大きく，胴体はずんどう型です。プロポーションは，全体的に
丸みをつけて描き，ポーズなども男女児の区別がありません。
子どもらしい可愛い雰囲気をだします。

Study exercises for drawing proportions

From three to five years old
Their heads are big and their bodies are cylindrical. Make the
proportions round in general. There are no distinctions between male
and female poses. Create childlike, cute moods.

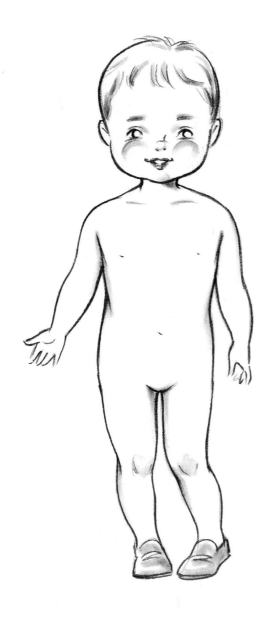

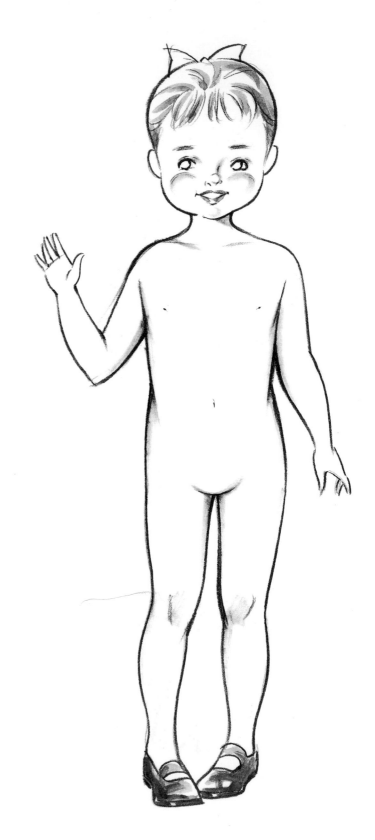

デザインなども可愛いらしいコスチュームで，おもちゃや，風船，帽子など小道具などを描き加えると，さらに子どもの雰囲気がでてきます。

Choose a costume cute in design and draw it adding small articles like balloons and hats to give it an even more childlike atmosphere.

●7才から10才

この年令は小生意気なおしゃまになってきます。ポーズも動きのある表情で描き，プロポーションも少し大人っぽくなってきています。

Study exercises in proportions
From seven to ten years of age

At this age children are becoming impertinent and precocious. Their proportions become a little more like adults. Draw expressive poses showing movement.

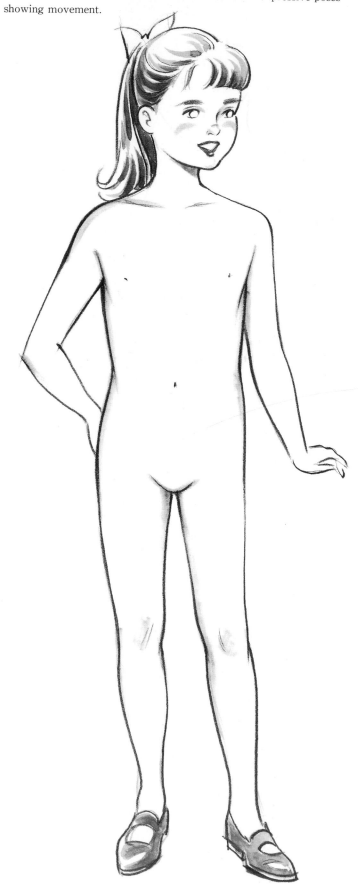

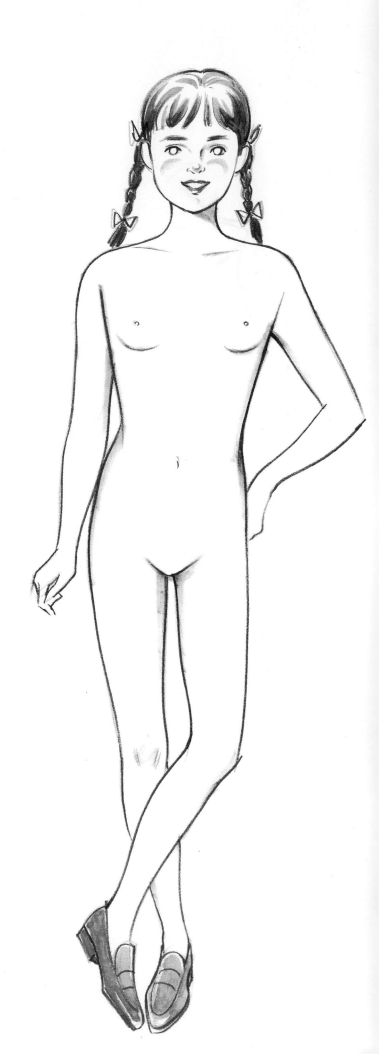

カジュアルなデザインとドレッシーなデザインコスチューム
ではポーズや動きによってデザインイメージが違ってきます。
ポーズのとり方にも注意しましょう。

Casual and dress clothing require different design images
because of differences in movement and posture. Pay close
attention to model's poses.

●15才から17才 From fifteen to seventeen years of age

プロポーションもほとんど大人に近づいてきています。
ポーズも少し大人っぽく描きます。

From the ages of fifteen to seventeen children's proportions are almost the same as adults'. Draw them more like adults.

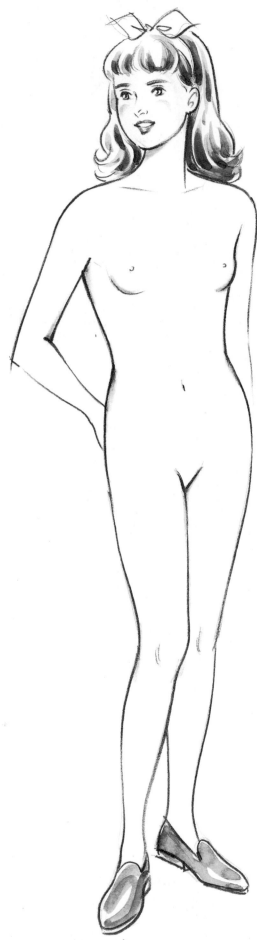

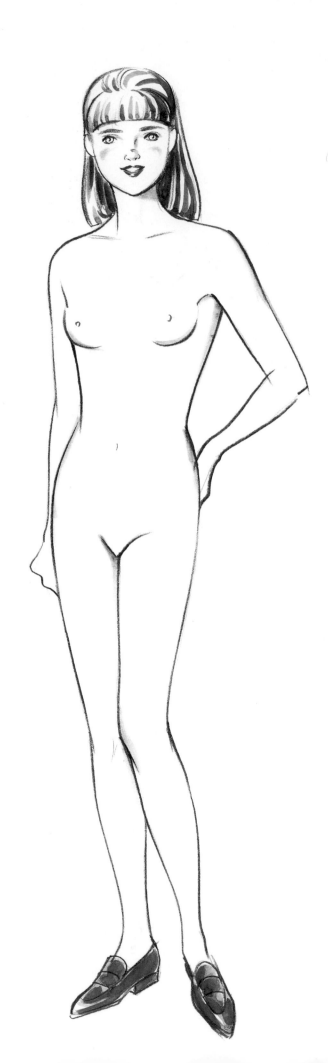

ポーズも大人と同じように基本的にはS字型に描いた方が，棒立ち
のポーズより動きもでて，全体のイメージが美しく見えます。

Their poses should be basically drawn in an S shape like that of
adults. Use more postures other than standing upright and make their
overall image more beautiful.

重心の軸脚

立ちポーズのとき大切なことは，ポーズがしっかりと立っているかどうかを確めて下さい。
身体が傾いて意外と倒れそうなポーズがよくあります。そのようなポーズを直すには，ま
ずどちらの脚に体重が乗っているかをよく見て下さい。
腰が動いて出ている方に体重が移動しますので，体重がかかっている脚が必ず，軸脚に
なります。そのとき，首の中心線の真下近くに，軸脚のかかとがきます。

Axial Leg

In the case of standing poses it is essential that the figure stands steadily and firmly. You often
see poses that tilt as if the figure is falling. To correct this, first study closely on which leg
the weight of the body rests. One's weight naturally shifts to the leg of an thrust hip. This is
referred to as the axial leg. The heel of the axial leg should always be drawn directly below
the center line of the neck.

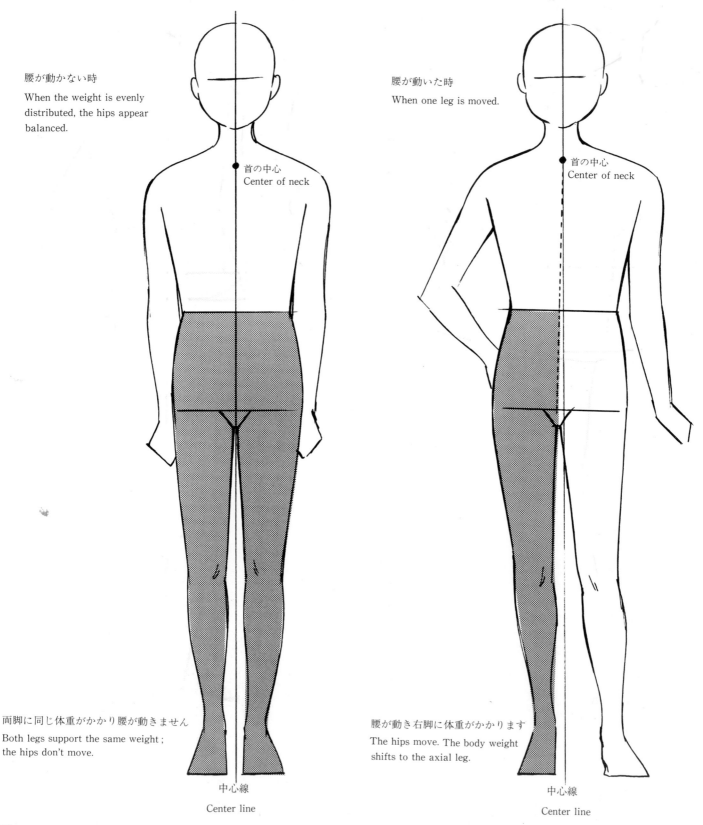

腰が動かない時

When the weight is evenly
distributed, the hips appear
balanced.

首の中心
Center of neck

腰が動いた時

When one leg is moved.

首の中心
Center of neck

両脚に同じ体重がかかり腰が動きません

Both legs support the same weight;
the hips don't move.

腰が動き右脚に体重がかかります

The hips move. The body weight
shifts to the axial leg.

中心線

Center line

中心線

Center line

腰が動き体重が脚に移動します

The hips move.

The weight of the body shifts to the axial leg.

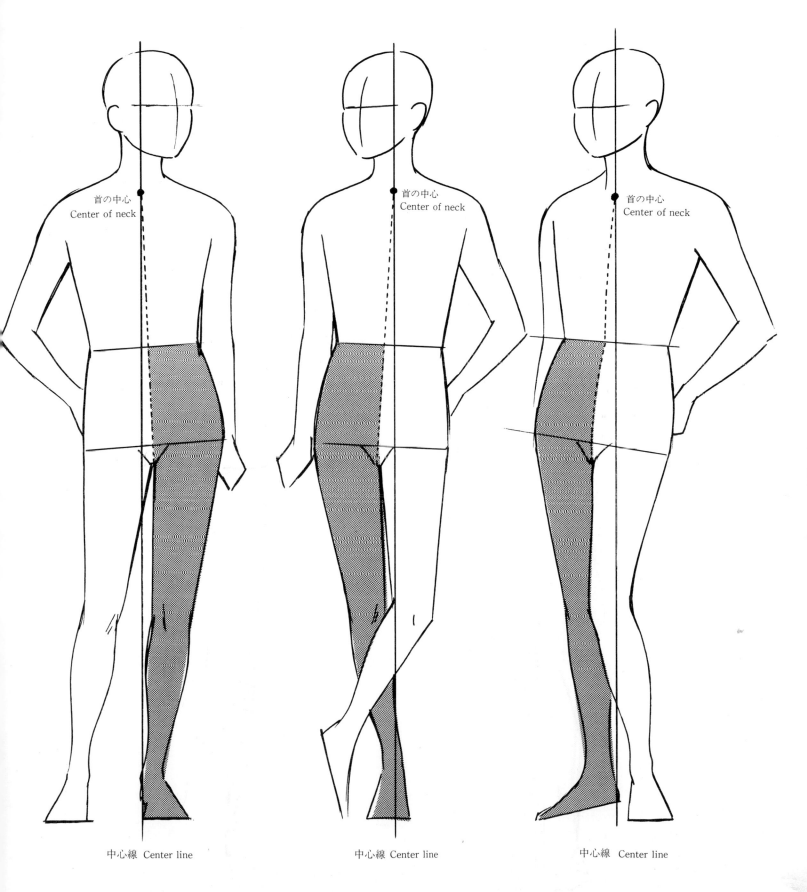

首の中心
Center of neck

首の中心
Center of neck

首の中心
Center of neck

中心線 Center line

中心線 Center line

中心線 Center line

左脚に体重がかかります

The left leg supports the weight of the body.

右脚に体重がかかります

The right leg supports the weight.

右脚に体重がかかります

The right leg supports the body weight.

プロポーション＆
コスチュームの関係

The relationship between proportions and costumes

身体の動きによって，コスチュームが身体にフィットする部分と，
離れる部分があります。
デザインによって，スリムなコスチュームとビッグなコスチューム
によっても違ってきます。描く時に，自分でポーズをとって研究し
てみましょう。

Some parts of the costume fit to the body and other parts don't depending on the body's movement. There are also differences between tight and loose clothes. When you draw, pose before a mirror and study closely.

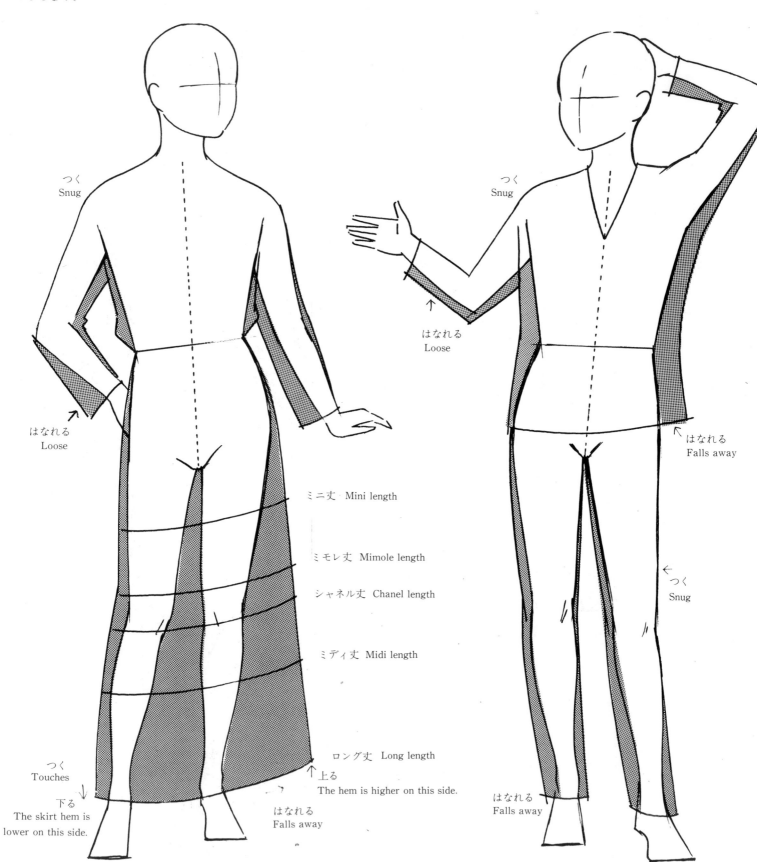

つく
Snug

はなれる
Loose

ミニ丈 Mini length

ミモレ丈 Mimole length

シャネル丈 Chanel length

ミディ丈 Midi length

ロング丈 Long length

つく
Touches

↓下る
The skirt hem is
lower on this side.

↑上る
The hem is higher on this side.

はなれる
Falls away

つく
Snug

はなれる
Loose

はなれる
Falls away

つく
Snug

はなれる
Falls away

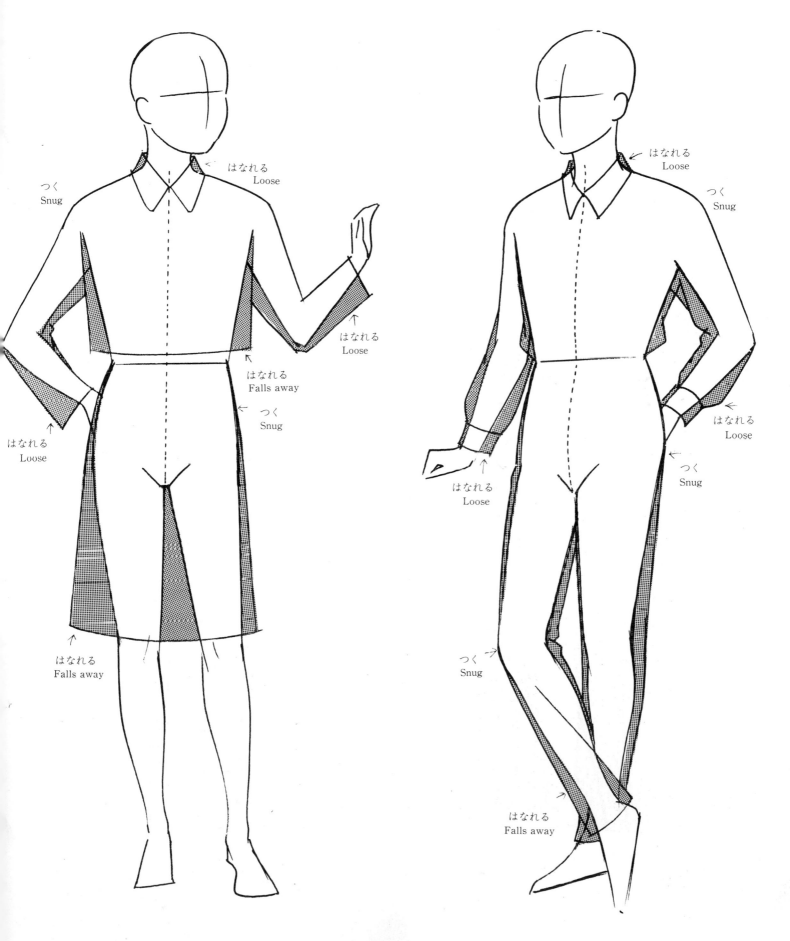

はなれる
Loose

つく
Snug

はなれる
Loose

はなれる
Loose

はなれる
Falls away

つく
Snug

はなれる
Loose

はなれる
Falls away

はなれる
Loose

つく
Snug

つく
Snug

はなれる
Falls away

コスチューム・パターン画の描き方

全身のファッション画を描くのが得意でないという人は，まずコスチュームをパターン画に描けるように勉強して下さい。
この描き方が描けるようになりましたら，洋服だけを上下着た状態に描き，顔，手，脚をシルエットで描き入れれば，全体のデザインのイメージがさらによく解ります。

How to draw costume patterns

If you are still inexperienced at drawing fashion illustrations using full length figures, begin by studying how to draw clothes patterns. Draw the top and bottom of the costume and add the face, arms and legs in silhouette. This makes the design more complete.

❶パターン画を描きます。
Draw the costume patterns first.

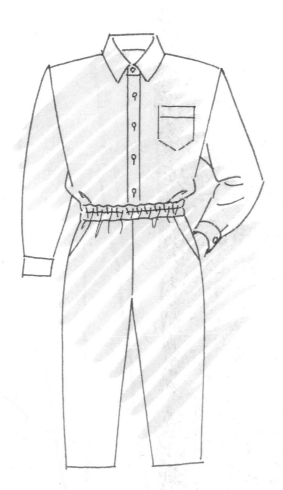

❷着せた状態に描きます。
Draw the costume patterns as clothes molded to a body.

❸顔，ヘア，手，脚を描き，全体のデザインイメージが
パターン画と違っていることに気がつきます。

Adding the face, hair, hands and legs will change the costume patterns into design images.

❶最初はパターン画を描きます。
Draw the pattern of the costume first.

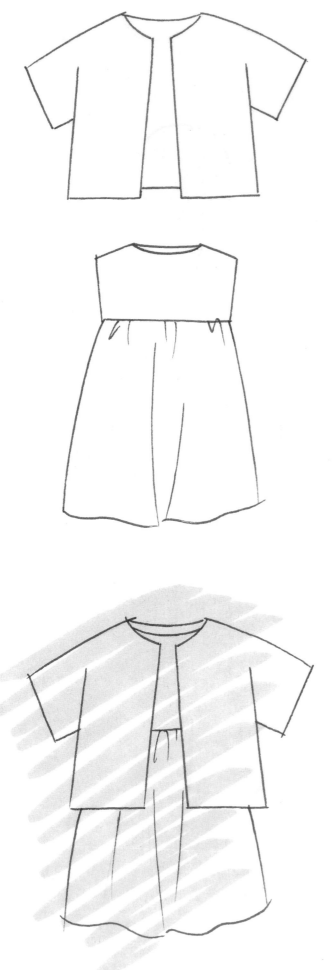

❷着せた状態に描きます。
Draw the pattern as clothes.

❸顔，ヘア，手，脚を描き入れます。パターン画のイラストよりもデザインのイメージ，着丈などがはっきりと見えてきます。

Add the face, hair, arms and legs. Now you can grasp the design and the length of clothes more clearly than you do with the costume patterns.

❶パターン画に描きます。
Draw the costume patterns.

❷着せた状態に描きます。

Draw them again as clothes.

❸着た状態に顔，ヘア，手，脚を描き入れ雰囲気をだ
します。

Create mood by adding a face, hair, hands and legs.

コスチュームの部分練習

Practicing on the individual parts

デザイン画を描く時，衿の型やボタン位置は意外に解りにくいものです。ポケット，しわ，スカート，パンツなどを描く時には，部分的な基礎をよく観察して描いてみましょう。

In illustrating designs, one sometimes suddenly finds oneself unable to draw details such as the collar shape, the location of buttons, pockets, wrinkles, the shape of skirts and pants. Practice these.

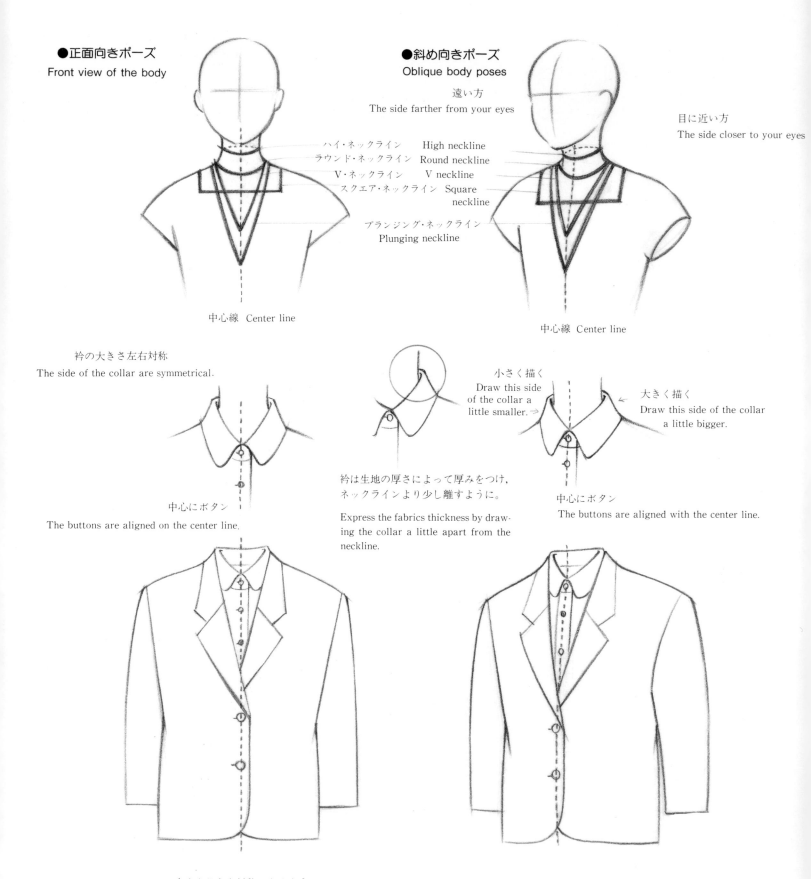

● 正面向きポーズ
Front view of the body

● 斜め向きポーズ
Oblique body poses

遠い方
The side farther from your eyes

目に近い方
The side closer to your eyes

ハイ・ネックライン　High neckline
ラウンド・ネックライン　Round neckline
V・ネックライン　V neckline
スクエア・ネックライン　Square neckline
プランジング・ネックライン
Plunging neckline

中心線　Center line

中心線　Center line

衿の大きさ左右対称
The side of the collar are symmetrical.

小さく描く
Draw this side of the collar a little smaller.

大きく描く
Draw this side of the collar a little bigger.

衿は生地の厚さによって厚みをつけ，ネックラインより少し離すように。

Express the fabrics thickness by drawing the collar a little apart from the neckline.

中心にボタン
The buttons are aligned on the center line.

中心にボタン
The buttons are aligned with the center line.

中心より左右対称になるように
Draw the left half and the right half equidistant from the center line.

中心より6対4の比率になるように
Draw the body's left and right sides with a ratio of 6:4 from the center line.

ファッションイラストでは，しわを描くことは大変重要なことです。生地の材質感や，身体の動き，ボディの立体感を表わすのになくてはならない描き方です。

多く描きすぎても，デザインの美しさが損なわれますので描きすぎに注意しなければなりません。曲げたところのくびれから，身体の高いところにコスチュームがフィットしている方へ，しわが曲線にできます。よく観察して描いてみましょう。

How to draw gathers and wrinkles

Knowing how to accurately draw gathers and wrinkles in fabric is very important in fashion illustration. Portraying the wrinkled surfaces of fabric will enable you to express the movement of the body, the texture and feel of the cloth and give a three dimensional appearance to fabrics. Take care to avoid drawing so many wrinkles and gathers that they spoil the beauty of the design. Fabric gathers where the arm is bent. Wrinkles run toward the upper part of the area where clothes tighten. Study them closely, and draw them.

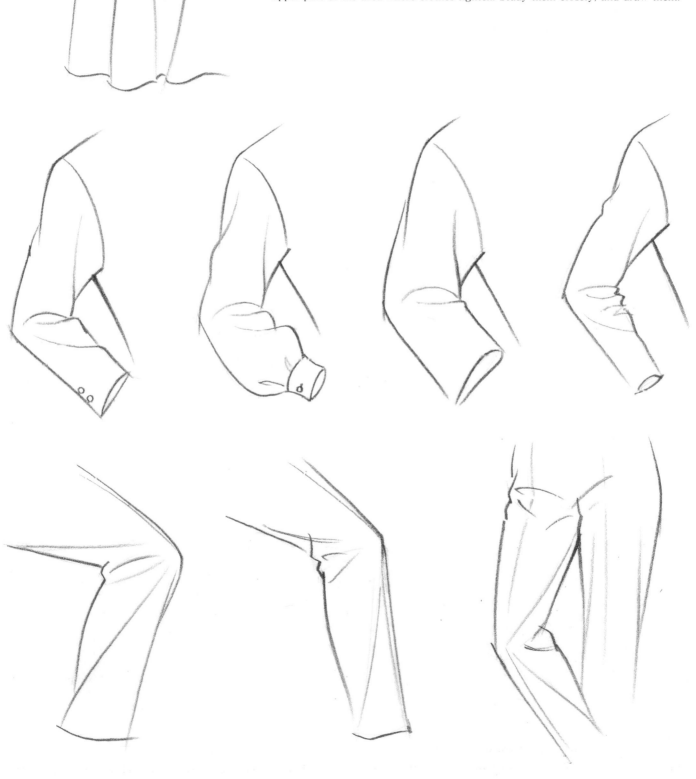

スカートの描き方

スカートの種類もたくさんありますが、デザイン機能をしっかりとらえて描きましょう。
デザイン上つくられたギャザー、プリーツなどのしわと、ポーズ（動き）によってできるしわとは性質が異なりますので注意しましょう。動きによるしわは、できるだけ省略し、あまり強調しないようにあっさりと描き表わします。

How to draw skirts

There are many kinds of skirts. Draw them by fully grasping their design and function. Gathers, pleats and wrinkles made by design rather than movement are treated differently. Avoid drawing too many wrinkles due to body movement. Don't emphasize them.

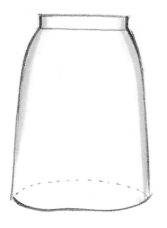

セミタイト
Semi-tight

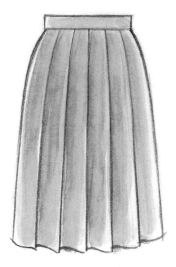

プリーツスカート
Pleated skirt

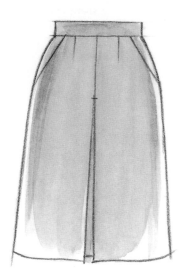

インバーステッド・スカート
Inverted pleat skirt

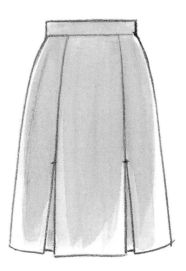

ボックスプリーツ・スカート
Box pleat skirt

フレアースカート
Flared skirt

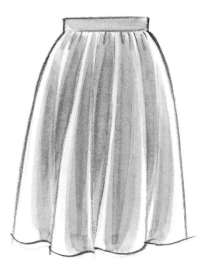

ギャザースカート
Gathered skirt

レィアード・スカート
Layered skirt

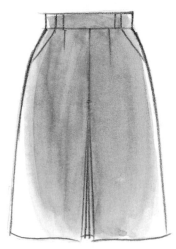

キュロットスカート
Culotte skirt

タイトスカート
Tight skirt

パンツの描き方

パンツの場合は，脚にフィットしている部分と離れている部分をよく理解し，動きによるしわのでる部分はどこにでるかなど，よく研究して描いて下さい。

How to draw pants

In order to draw pants, understand where pants fit closely or loosely to the leg, where they hang away from the leg, and where wrinkles appear.

ショートパンツ　Short pants

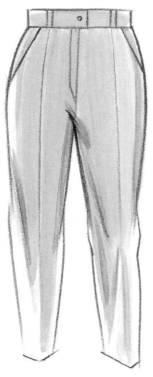

ストレートパンツ　Straight pants

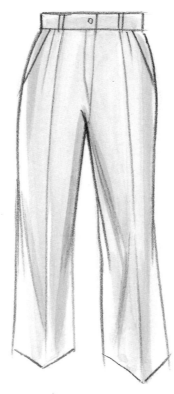

パンタロン　Pantaloons

ジーンズ　Jeans

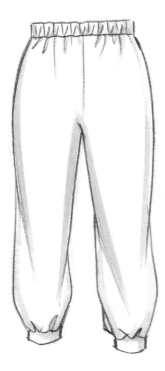

ペッグ・パンツ　Peg pants

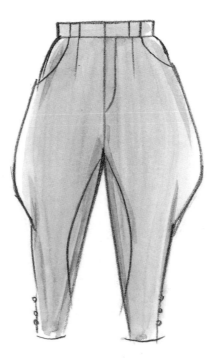

ジョッパーズ　Jodhpurs

レオタード　Leotard

柄の描き方

最初はできるだけ省略しないで丁寧に描きましょう。ダーツやディテールなど
デザインが解るように,その部分は淡く描くか,だんだん省略して描きましょう。

How to draw the patterns in fabrics

At first draw the patterns in full omitting no details. As you become experienced
you can gradually omit details. Draw patterns thinner or omit them where they go
across darts or other costume design details.

子どもの描き方

年齢別の描き方
画材によるテクニック
素材の描き方
描き方のバリエーション

How to draw children

How to draw children of different ages

Techniques using various media

How to draw fabric

Variations

０才〜３才の描き方

生れた時から3才ぐらいまでは、頭が大きく動きも不安定で、ぎごちない動作が小さい子どもの可愛らしさをひきたたせます。

親としてこの年令は、目に入れてもいたくないと言います。全体に顔、手、足はふっくらと丸く描きます。

How to draw children from less than a year old to age three

Children from newly born up to the age of three years old have big heads and their movements are unstable. Their awkwardness in behavior makes little children seem very cute. Children of this age are said to be the apples of their parents' eyes. In general draw their faces, arms and legs plump and round.

画用紙●エボニー鉛筆●透明水彩

Ebony pencil and transparent watercolor on paper.

画用紙●エボニー鉛筆●透明水彩

Ebony pencil and transparent watercolor on paper.

ケント紙●エボニー鉛筆●透明水彩

Ebony pencil and transparent watercolor on Kent paper.

ケント紙●ボールペン●マーカー●サインペン●パステル

Ball-point pen, marker, felt-tip pen and pastel on Kent paper.

5才〜7才の描き方

この年令になってくると，プロポーションもスマートになってきます。

ポーズは，健康的で活発な動きのある小生意気な感じを出します。この年ごろは，遊びにもなんでも一番興味を持ち，おしゃれに対してもうるさくなります。

How to draw children from five to seven years of age

At these ages children's proportions have become slimmer. When you draw their poses, emphasize their saucy air with healthy and lively movements. Children in this stage are most interested in whatever they see and have become particular about their appearance.

ケント紙●パステル鉛筆●パステル●透明水彩●カラートーン

Pastel pencil, pastel, transparent watercolor and colortone on Kent paper.

ケント紙●サインペン●透明水彩

Felt-tip pen and trnsparent watercolor on Kent paper.

ケント紙●サインペン●カラートーン

Felt-tip pen and colortone on Kent paper.

画用紙●パステル鉛筆●ポスターカラー●パステル

Pastel pencil, poster color and pastel on paper.

10才〜12才の描き方

この年令は脚や身体つきが大人のプロポーションに似てきます。可愛らしさはまだありますが、少し大人っぽく描きます。ファッションも少し大人っぽくキザになってきます。

How to draw children from ten to twelve years of age

These children's legs, frame and constitution have become close to that of adults. They are still cute, but draw them rather a bit like adults. Their fashion becomes a little mature and conceited.

ケント紙●エボニー鉛筆●クレヨン●透明水彩

Ebony pencil, crayon and transparent watercolor on Kent paper.

ケント紙●色鉛筆●パステル

Colored pencil and pastel on Kent paper.

ケント紙●エボニー鉛筆●透明水彩●パステル

Ebony pencil, transparent watercolor and pastel on Kent paper.

15才～17才の描き方

プロポーションは大人と変りませんが，顔の
描き方で大人との違いを出します。
ファッションもポーズも少し大人っぽく描き
ます。

How to draw young adults from age fifteen to seventeen

Their proportions are different from that of adults, but you show the difference between the two in the way you draw the faces. Draw their fashion and poses more adult-like.

画用紙●パステル鉛筆●透明水彩

Pastel pencil and transparent watercolor on paper.

画用紙 ●パステル鉛筆 ●透明水彩 ●色鉛筆

*Pastel pencil, transparent watercolor and
colored pencil on paper.*

49

Techniques using various mediums

鉛筆&水彩

鉛筆画と水彩着彩の描き方は，ごく一般的な描き方です。イラスト
を描きはじめの人は，この描き方が抵抗なく自然に描けるでしょう。

Pencils and Watercolors

Drawing in pencil and coloring with watercolors is the most natural
way to illustrate. It should be the easiest way offering the fewest
difficulties for beginning illustrators.

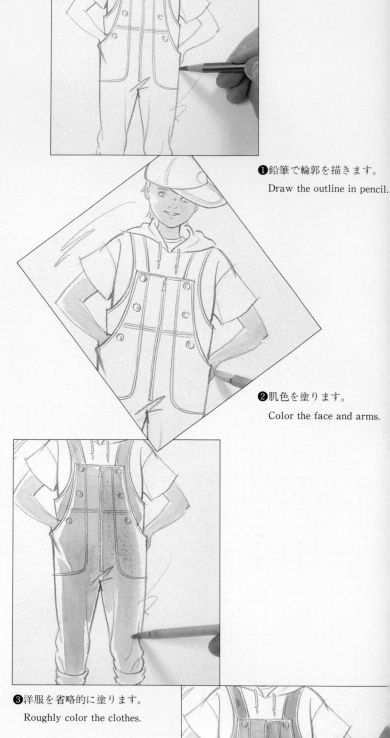

❶鉛筆で輪郭を描きます。
Draw the outline in pencil.

❷肌色を塗ります。
Color the face and arms.

❸洋服を省略的に塗ります。
Roughly color the clothes.

❹省略に塗った端の方をグラデーションをつけてぼかします。
Gradate the edges of the color.

仕上り
Finished

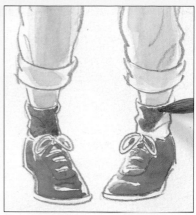

❺シャツを塗ります。

Paint the shirt.

❻帽子もシャツの色を塗ります。

Add to the cap the same color as that of the shirt.

❼靴に色を塗ります。

Paint the shoes.

❽洋服の色に合せて靴下に色を入れます。

Color the socks to match the clothes.

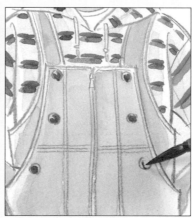

❾シャツにストライプを筆で描き入れます。

With a brush add stripes to the shirt.

❿ストライプの色違いの色を描き入れます。

Add stripes of a different color.

⓫ボタンに色をつけます。

Paint the buttons.

⓬唇に色をさします。

Color the lips.

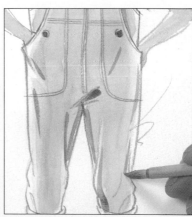

⓭ほゝに擦筆で色をさします。

Color the cheeks with a stump.

⓮ひとみを塗ります。

Paint in the pupils of the eyes.

⓯ひとみとほゝの光をポスターカラーの白で入れます。

High light the cheeks and add light to the eyes with poster color white.

⓰最後に全体に影を同系色の濃い色で描き入れます。

At last, put in shadows with darker shades of the same colors.

Techniques using various mediums
色鉛筆＆パステル

パステル画は全体のイメージとしてホットな雰囲気ですから，あまり描き込まず軽いタッチで描き上げます。

Colored Pencils and Pastels
Generally pastels create a heavy mood, so don't paint too many details and finish with a light touch.

❶画用紙に肌色のパステルを塗り，擦筆で色を混ぜ合せ自分の好きな肌色を作ります。

Paint various skin tones on paper with pastel ; blend them with stump to find your favorite skin color.

❷最初は力を入れずに擦筆で肌の色を塗っていきます。

Paint the skin with the stump using a lignt touch at first.

❸顔やヘアのように小さい面のところは，擦筆に色をつけて塗ります。

When painting small areas like the face and hair, put color on the stump and paint.

仕上り
Completed

 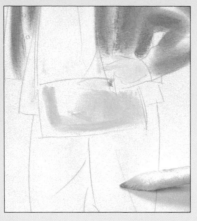 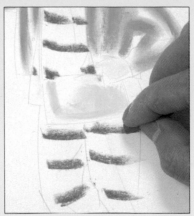 

④洋服は，輪郭やしわの部分に色を塗り指でのばしグラデーションにぼかします。

In the case of clothes, add color to the outline and wrinkles; spread and gradate it with a finger.

⑤シャツやボトムの明るい色は擦筆で塗ります。

Paint the bright colors of shirts and pants with a stump.

⑥シャツやボトムの柄は，パステルを直に描き入れます。

Add the patterns of the shirt and lower half.

⑦色を全部塗り終えたら，色鉛筆で輪郭を描き入れます。

When you finish coloring everything, draw the outline in colored pencil.

   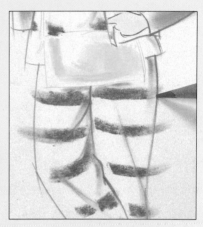

❽輪郭の線は同じ色だけでなく，濃い色や違う色を入れ，めりはりを出します。

Draw the outline not only with the same color, but also with darker shades or different colors giving dark and light tones.

❾顔やヘアの輪郭を描き入れます。トップの輪郭を上から下へと描き入れます。

After drawing the outline of the face, draw the outline of the top of the outfit working from the top down.

❿輪郭は洋服と同じ色か同系色で描きます。

In drawing the outline, draw it with the same color as the clothes in the same or another shade.

⓫ボトムの輪郭にもめりはりをつけます。

Add contrasting tones to the outline of the lower half.

⓬全体を見て，最後に濃いところを描き入れます。

Going over the entire picture, add color to the darkest areas of the outline to finish.

⓭雰囲気を出すために，バックに色をつけます。

Color in the background to create atmosphere.

⓮バックに入れた色を指でぼかします。

Gradate the color of the background with your finger.

⓯最後にパステルを定着させるために，定着剤スプレーをかけます。

Finally, spray with fixative to fix the pastels.

Techniques using various mediums
サインペン＆カラートーン

カラートーンを切り張りします。この方法は色が平面的なので、やややもするとぬり絵的になりやすいので、色を張るときに、省略的にしたり、重ねるなどして、めりはりを付けて仕上げましょう。

Felt-tip pen and Colortone

When using felt-tip pen and colortone, make the picture by cutting and placing the colortone media. Since colortone colors are flat, the picture tends to look one-dimensional, therefore, place the colortone irregularly, or make some parts doubletone and finish out the overall picture with contrasting tones.

❶口，ほゝに色を入れます。

Color the lips and cheeks.

❷カラートーンを肌よりやゝ大きめに切ります。

Cut out the colortone and trim it to a size larger than that of the face.

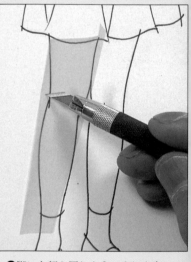

❸切り張りし，カラートーンをカットして肌に色を入れます。

Apply the colortone and trim it to the exact size. Cut out the eyes and eyebrows and paint them. Tint the cheeks.

❹脚にも顔と同じように入れます。

Apply the colortone to the legs in the same way as you did the face.

仕上り
Completed

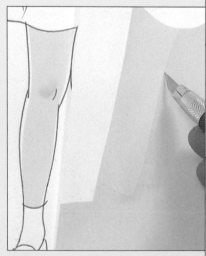

❺カラートーンを脚に合せてカットします。

Cut the colortone to the approximate size of the legs.

❻ヘアにカラートーンを張ります。

Place colortone for the hair.

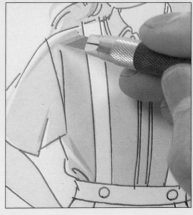

❼ヘアの色を張ったら, ヘアの流れをダブらせます。

After placing the hair color, use doubletone for the flow of the hairstyle and contrasting shades of color.

❽洋服に色を入れ, カットしていきます。

Cut out the colortone for the blouse and add it.

❾洋服も単調にならないようにします。

Add contrasting tones to the blouse to avoid monotony.

❿スカートに色を張り, カットします。

Place the colortone for the skirt and trim it.

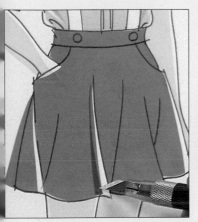

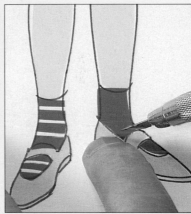

⓫しわには, カラートーンをダブらせて張ります。

Use doubletone to make wrinkles.

⓬しわのところをカットして, 省略して張ります。

Cut out the wrinkles and place the colortone irregularly.

⓭靴下に色を張ります。

Use colortone for the socks.

⓮柄のストライプをカットして, はがしていきます。

Cut out the stripes and peel them off.

⓯リボンにストライプを入れます。

Trim out the stripes of the ribbons as with the socks.

⓰全体に動きが出るようにバックに色をとばします。

Add a little color to the background to give a sense of movement to the picture.

⓱ほ, の光をポスターカラーの白で入れます。

Highlight the cheeks with poster color white.

⓲洋服にも白で水玉の柄を入れます。

Add white polka dots to the blouse.

55

Techniques using various mediums
筆ペン＆ポスターカラー

ポスターカラーの塗り方も平面的になりやすいので、色を省略的に塗り立体感を出します。アウトラインを出来るだけ強弱の出る筆ペンで描きます。

Brush Pencil and Poster Colors

Painting in poster color tends to give a picture a flat surface, so draw the outline as much as possible in brush pen which can create contrasting light and dark tones and paint roughly to give the feel of three dimensions.

❶筆ペンで出来るだけ強弱をつけて、輪郭を描きます。

Draw the outline in brush pencil, giving as much variation in dark and light tones as possible.

❷肌色を描いた上から塗ります。

Color the skin.

❸ヘアを塗ります。

Add color to the hair.

❹少しグラデーションにぼかします。

Gradate the edges of the colors.

❺ジャケットは輪郭の線を消さないように省略に色を塗ります。

Rough in the color of the jacket being careful not to erase the outline.

仕上り

Completed

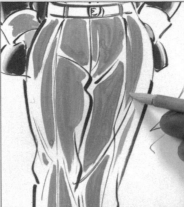

❻色を塗った端をグラデーションにぼかします。

Gradate the color to the edges.

❼ボトムも省略に塗ります。

Rough in the pants as you did the jacket.

❽色を塗った端をグラデーションにぼかします。

Gradate the color to the edges.

❾靴に色をつけます。

Paint the shoes.

❿肌色を塗って消えた目や鼻，口を描き入れます。

Draw the eyes, nose and mouth which were erased when painting the skintones.

⓫唇に色を差します。

Add in color for the lips.

⓬ほゝに色を入れます。

Color the cheeks.

⓭目やほゝの光っているところに，ポスターカラーの白を入れます。

Highlight the eyes and the cheeks with white poster color.

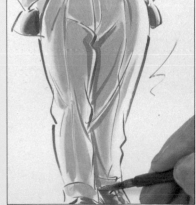

⓮チョウタイに柄を入れます。

Add the patterns of the bow tie.

⓯ジャケットに影を入れます。

Add shadows to the jacket.

⓰シャツに色を塗ります。

Paint the shirt.

⓱ボトムにも影を入れます。

Add shadows to the bottom and the picture is complete.

Techniques using various mediums
サインペン＆マーカー

マーカーで仕上げるのは短時間で出来て便利ですが，紙質によっては，にじんだり，むらが出来てきれいに仕上らないことがあります。マーカー専門用紙のマーカーパット紙を使用すれば最適です。

Felt-tip Pens and Markers
Using Markers has the advantage that you can finish the picture in a short time. But markers blur and paint unevenly depending on the quality of paper you use. If possible, it is best to use marker pad paper especially made for use with markers sold by Letraset.

❶サインペンで輪郭をとります。それから肌色を塗ります。

Color the skin after drawing the outline in felt-tip pen.

❷ヘアに省略的に色を塗ります。

Roughly paint in the hair.

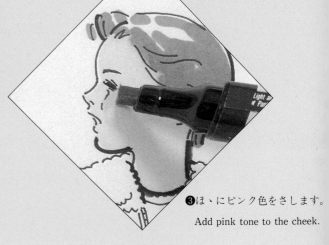

❸ほ丶にピンク色をさします。

Add pink tone to the cheek.

仕上り

Finished

❹洋服に色をつけます。ペンタッチを出来るだけ同じ方向に塗ります。

When coloring the top try always to paint in the same direction.

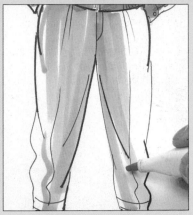

⑤塗り終ってから、同じ色でしわや影をつけます。

After painting, use the same color to add wrinkles and shadows.

⑥ボトムに色をつけます。外側を省略的に塗りましょう。

Paint the bottom half roughly, especially the outside.

⑦重ね塗りをしますと、初めに塗った色より濃くなり、影の効果がでます。

Color the pants again with the same color. Naturally the painted over part is a darker shade. It gives the effect of shadows.

⑧ボアを塗ります。

Color the boa.

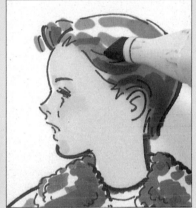

⑨少し濃い色を入れ、ボアの雰囲気を出します。

Add a little darker color to give the boa atmosphere.

⑩濃い色でヘアの流れや、めりはりをつけます。

Add dark color to give contrast and show the flow of the hair.

⑪ボトムにチェックの柄を描き入れます。

Add a loud checkered pattern to the pants.

⑫⑪と同じ

Continuation of figure 11

⑬ボトムの影やしわを濃く入れます。

With a darker tone add shadows and wrinkles.

⑭トップにも濃い影やしわを入れます。

Add the darkest shadows and wrinkles at the top.

⑮バックにタッチを入れ動きを出します。

Add a few touches to the background to suggest movement.

⑯ほゝの光をポスターカラーの白で入れます。

Highlight the cheek in white poster color.

How to Draw Fabrics
ニットの描き方

ニットの風合いを出すには，画用紙にクレヨンやパステルで描くの
が適しています。編地を表現するには，色鉛筆などがよいでしょう。

How to draw knits

A good way to express the feel and appearance of knits is to draw on
drawing paper with crayon and pastels and to use colored pencils to
draw the mesh.

❶鉛筆で輪郭を描きます。
Draw the outline in pencil.

❷水彩で肌色を塗ります。
Paint the skin tone with watercolor.

❸クレヨンでセーターの柄を描き入れ
ます。
Add the patterns of the sweater with
crayons.

❹白の柄はローソクを使います。
Make the white pattern with wax.

仕上り
Completed

❺セーター，マフラー，帽子などにクレ
ヨンで柄を描き入れます。

Use crayon for the patterns of the
sweater, muffler and cap.

❻柄を描き入れた地の色は，水彩を筆に
たっぷりつけて塗ります。

Use a brush soaked in red to color the
ground.

❼水彩で塗るとクレヨンで描いた柄が，
水をはじいて浮き出てきます。

The part done in crayon repels the
watercolor, so the patterns stand out.

❽少し水を含ませた筆で，色の端をグラ
デーションにぼかします。

Gradate the edges of colors with a wet
brush soaked in a little water.

❾マフラーもセーターと同じ塗り方をし
ます。

Paint the muffler in the same way as
you did the sweater.

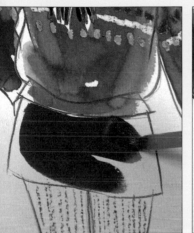

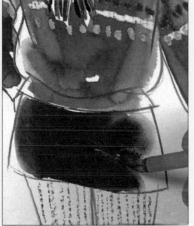

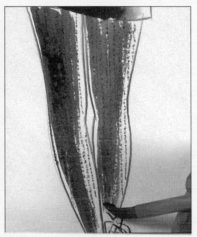

❿スカートも省略に塗ります。

Rough in the skirt color.

⓫色の端をグラデーションにぼかします。

Add gradation to the edges of the color.

⓬タイツを塗ります。

Color the tights.

⓭唇に色をさします。

Paint the lips.

⓮ほゝに擦筆で赤味の色をつけます。

Add color to the cheeks with stump.

⓯目の光やほゝにポスターカラーの白で
描き入れます。

Highlight the eyes and cheeks in white
poster color with a brush.

⓰バックに水彩でタッチを入れます。

Touch up the background with watercolor.

⓱セーターのゴム編みを，色鉛筆で描き
入れます。

Use colored pencil to draw the weave of
the sweater.

How to Draw Fabrics
毛皮の描き方

長い毛足のコートを表現するには，画用紙にクレヨンを使い，水彩
で色づけします。この描き方がもっとも簡単です。

How to draw fur.
The easiest way to draw long fur is with crayon and watercolor on
drawing paper.

❶肌色はマーカーを使います。
Use marker for skin color.

❷ヘアもマーカーで塗ります。
Color the hair with marker also

仕上り
The completed sketch.

❸クレヨンで毛足の流れを描き込みます。
Draw the texture of long fur with
crayon.

❹毛足の濃い部分に濃い色を入れます。
Use a different color to add the dark
shade of the fur.

⑤クレヨンで描いた上に，太い筆を使い
　水彩で色を塗ります。

Paint the coat with a wide brush in watercolor after you have drawn it in crayon.

⑥スーツのツイードはクレヨンで描き入れます。

Add the tweed texture of the suit in crayon.

⑦スーツにも水彩で色を塗ります。

Paint the suit in watercolor.

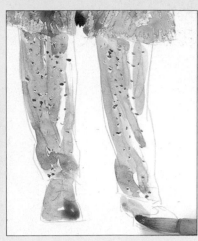

⑧靴に色を塗ります。

Color the shoes.

⑨毛足の流れが少なければ，筆で描きた
　します。

If the flow of the fur is not expressed well enough, add more with a brush.

⑩渇きが遅ければドライヤーを使います。

If the picture doesn't dry quickly, use a hair dryer.

⑪口に色をさします。

Color the lips.

⑫鉛筆で輪郭を入れます。

Do the outline in pencil.

⑬輪郭を入れるときにイラストを汚さな
　いように，ペーパーなどを敷いて注意
　しましょう。

Take care when drawing the outline not to dirty the picture. Place a tissue under your hand.

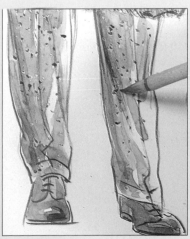

⑭全体に影やしわを描きます。

Add wrinkles and shadows as necessary.

⑮ボタンにポスターカラーの白で光を描
　き入れます。

Highlight the buttons with white postor color.

⑯雰囲気を出すためにバックに色を入れ
　ます。

To give an overall atmosphere to the picture, add color to the background.

How to Draw Fabrics
デニム&バックスキンの描き方

画用紙に水彩とパステルで仕上げます。バックスキンの表わし方は、擦筆にパステルをつけこすります。むらを出しながら仕上げていきます。

How to draw denim and buckskin

Do the picture in watercolor and pastels. To get the texture of buckskin, color a stump with pastels and roughen the texture of the clothes.

❶水彩で肌色を塗ります。

Add skin color to the face.

❷水彩でバックスキンのところを塗ります。

Color the buckskin in watercolor.

❸水彩を塗り終えたところ。

Do the same to the skirt with a brush.

仕上り
The completed sketch.

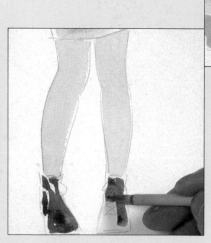

❹デニムのところに水彩で色をつけます。

Color the denim part in watercolor.

❺タイツと靴に色を入れます。

Paint the tights and shoes.

❻画用紙にパステルを塗り，擦筆に色を
つけます。

Color the drawing paper with pastels and soak the stump with color.

❼擦筆でバックスキンにむらを出しなが
ら塗ります。

Texture the buckskin with the stump.

❽擦筆に濃い色をつけ，濃いところを描
き込んでいきます。

Soak the stump with a darker color and paint in the darker shade of color.

❾デニムの色をバックスキンと同じ方法
で塗ります。

Color and texture the denim with the stump as you did the buckskin.

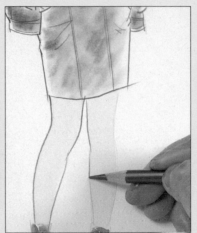

❿シャツを水彩で塗ります。

Paint the shirt in watercolor.

⓫鉛筆で輪郭を描き入れます。

Put in the outline with pencil.

⓬輪郭は上から下へ描き入れます。

When outlining, work from top to bottom.

⓭顔に影を入れます。

Shadow the face.

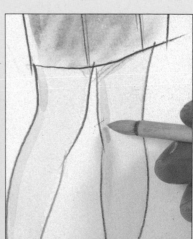

⓮口に色をさします。

Add color to the lips.

⓯ほゝに擦筆で色を入れます。

Color the cheeks with a stump.

⓰ボタンを塗ります。

Paint the buttons.

⓱影を入れ仕上げます。

Add shadows as needed to the overall sketch.

65

How to Draw Fabrics
ベルベットの描き方

ベルベットのように生地に光沢のあるものの表わし方は，ケント紙に水彩やポスターカラーなどでベタ塗りします。洋服の中の線が消えてしまいますので，消えた線や光っているところを，色鉛筆の明るい色で描き入れると，ベルベットの雰囲気がだせます。

How to draw velvet

To express a lustrous fabric like velvet, first draw the sketch in pencil on Kent paper, then paint over it evenly in watercolor or in poster color. Next, go over the lines and add the nap in a lighter shade of colored pencil. This method successfully captures the luster of velvet.

❶輪郭を鉛筆で描き，肌色から塗ります。
Draw the outline in pencil and start coloring the skin color.

仕上り
Finished

❷ヘアを塗ります。
Paint the hair.

❸洋服に色を塗ります。
Color the dress.

❹省略して塗ります。

When you paint the dress, paint roughly to the edges.

❺塗った端をグラデーションにぼかします。

After you paint, gradate the edges.

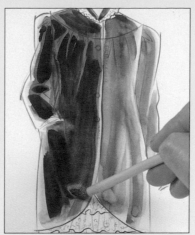

❻1回塗りでは淡いので，さらに重ね塗りをします。

One coat will not be dark enough, so paint it again.

❼重ね塗りしたところにも，端をグラデーションにぼかします。

When painting the second coat, gradate the edges as you did the first time.

❽スカートに色を塗ります。

Color the skirt.

❾靴に色をつけます。

Color the shoes.

❿リボンに色をつけます。

Add the ribbon color.

⓫口に色をさします。

Color the lips.

⓬ほゝに擦筆で色をつけます。

Add color to the cheeks with the stump.

⓭消えた輪郭線や光っている部分に，同系色の明るい色を，色鉛筆で描き入れます。

Redraw the lines covered by painting, the details and the lustrous velvet nap with a lighter colored pencil.

⓮明るいところは，色鉛筆の白で描き入れます。

Use a white colored pencil on the lighter parts.

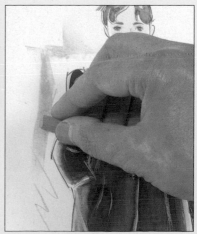

⓯バックをパステルでつけます。

Color the background in pastel.

How to Draw Fabrics

光沢のある毛皮の描き方

光沢のある毛皮や，ビニールコーティング生地などの表現には，
マーカーパット紙にマーカーで仕上げる方法が手軽で簡単です。

How to draw lustrous fur

The easy and simple way to draw a lustrous fur or a vinyl coated
fabric is to use marker on marker pad paper.

❶肌色を塗ります。

Color the skin.

❷ほ、に赤味をつけます。

Add a reddish color to the cheek

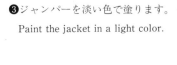

❸ジャンパーを淡い色で塗ります。

Paint the jacket in a light color.

❹全体に色をつけます。

First color it generally.

❺淡く塗った面より少なめに濃い色を塗ります。

Color the smaller area with a darker
color than the first.

仕上り

Completed

⑥その上に，濃い黒を塗ります。

Color over it with the darker color.

⑦マーカーのカラーブレンドで淡い色と濃い色を混ぜ合せ，グラデーションにぼかします。

Using marker color-blend, to blend light and dark colors and gradate to the edges.

⑧帽子もジャンパーと同じように色づけします。

Paint the beret as you did the jacket.

⑨サングラスも同じ塗り方です。

Color the sun glasses in the same way.

⑩パンツと靴を黒で塗ります。

Paint the pants and shoes in black.

⑪カラーブレンドで色の端を溶かしながら，グラデーションにぼかします。

Soften the edges of the color with color-blend and gradate to the edges.

⑫細書きのマーカーでボアの感じに描き入れます。

Paint the texture of the boa with a fine tip marker.

⑬口に色をさします。

Color the lips with a brush.

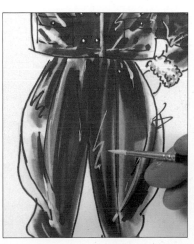

⑭輪郭をマーカーの細書き用で描き入れます。

Draw the outline with a fine tip marker.

⑮バックにタッチを入れます。

Give a few touches to the background.

⑯毛皮の光っているところに，ポスターカラーの白で描き入れます。

Paint the luster of the fur with white poster color and a brush.

⑰衿，袖口のボアに色をつけます。

Add color to the boa at the collar and the sleeves.

いろいろな描き方 *Various ways of drawing with different materials*

画用紙●エボニー鉛筆●透明水彩

Ebony pencil and transparent watercolor on paper.

ケント紙●ボールペン●透明水彩

Ball-point pen and transparent watercolor on Kent paper.

画用紙●エボニー鉛筆●透明水彩●ポスターカラー

Ebony pencil, transparent watercolor and poster color on paper.

ケント紙●サインペン●透明水彩●色鉛筆●擦筆

Felt-tip pen, transparent watercolor,
colored pencil and stump on Kent paper.

画用紙●エボニー鉛筆●透明水彩

Ebony pencil and transparent watercolor on paper.

画用紙●コンテ鉛筆●透明水彩●
パステル●ポスターカラー

*Conté, transparent watercolor, pastel
and poster color on paper.*

画用紙●サインペン●マーカー●ポスターカラー

Flet-tip pen, marker and poster color on paper.

画用紙●筆ペン●マーカー●パステル

Brush-pen, marker and pastel on paper.

画用紙 ●筆ペン●マーカー

Brush pen and marker on paper.

画用紙●ボールペン●マーカー

Ball-point pen and marker on paper.

画用紙●色鉛筆●パステル●マーカー

Colored pencil, pastel and marker on paper.

ケント紙●色鉛筆●パステル

Colored pencil and pastel on Kent paper.

ケント紙●マービーマーカー●パステル●色鉛筆

Marvymarker, pastel and colored pencil on Kent paper.

ケント紙●サインペン●カラートーン

Felt-tip pen and colortone on Kent paper.

ケント紙●サインペン●パステル

Felt-tip pen and pastel on Kent paper.

ケント紙●色鉛筆●パステル

Colored pencil and pastel on Kent paper.

ケント紙●色鉛筆

Colored pencil on Kent paper.

ケント紙 ●色鉛筆 ●パステル

Colored pencil and pastel on Kent paper.

ケント紙 ●色鉛筆 ●パステル

Colored pencil and pastel on Kent paper.

画用紙●色鉛筆●マーカー

Colored pencil and marker on paper.

ケント紙●エボニー鉛筆●水彩

Ebony pencil and water color on Kent paper.

画用紙●エボニー鉛筆●水彩

Ebony pencil and water color on paper.

ケント紙●サインペン●水彩

Felt-tip pen and water color on Kent paper.

ケント紙●サインペン●ポスターカラー

Felt-tip pen and poster color on Kent paper.

ント紙●サインペン●ポスターカラー

Felt-tip pen and poster color on Kent paper.

ケント紙●エボニー鉛筆●水彩

Ebony pencil and water color on Kent paper.

画用紙●エボニー鉛筆●クレヨン●水彩

Ebony pencil, crayon and water color on paper.

ケント紙 ●エボニー鉛筆 ●水彩

Ebony pencil and water color on Kent paper.

ケント紙●エボニー鉛筆●マーカー

Ebony pencil and marker on Kent paper.

マーカーパット●色鉛筆●マーカー

Colored pencil and marker on Marker Pad.

ケント紙●エボニー鉛筆●色鉛筆●水彩

Ebony pencil, colored pencil and water color on Kent paper.

マーカーパット●ボールペン●マーカー

Ball-point pen and marker on Marker Pad.

マーカーパット●エボニー鉛筆●マーカー

Ebony pencil and marker on Marker Pad.

マーカーパット●色鉛筆●パステル●マーカー

Colored pencil, pastel and marker on Marker Pad.

画用紙●サインペン●マーカー●パステル

Flet-tip pen, marker and pastel on paper.

スーツ

ファッションイラストを描く場合，重要なことのひとつ
にコスチュームデザインを的確に表現できることです。
いろいろと種類が多いデザインを描き分けることは大変
難しいことのように感じますが，デザインの持つルール
を知れば，それほど難しいことではありません。
それぞれコスチュームの持つムード，形，柄，材質感な
どよく見て，研究しながら描いてみましょう。

Suits

One of the important aspects of fashion illustration is that
of drawing designs with exactness. Drawing a wide range
of varied designs seems very difficult, but it is not so
difficult if you know the rules of design. Look carefully at
the mood, shape, patterns and textures of each costume
and study them well while drawing.

いろいろなコスチュームの描き方

How to draw various costumes

画用紙●エボニー鉛筆●水彩

Ebony pencil and water color on paper.

ケント紙●サインペン●マーカー

Felt-tip pen and marker on Kent paper.

画用紙●エボニー鉛筆●水彩

Ebony pencil and water color on paper.

ケント紙●サインペン●パステル●スクリーントーン

Felt-tip pen, pastel and screen tone on Kent paper.

画用紙●マーカー

Marker on paper.

ジャケット

スーツなどよりカジュアルなので，ポーズにも動きを出して，のび
のびとタッチも入れて描いてみましょう。

Jackets

Jackets are more casual than suits. Draw loosely allowing more
movement in poses with added touches.

ケント紙●エボニー鉛筆●マーカー

Ebony pencil and marker on Kent paper.

ケント紙●サインペン●マーカー

Felt-tip pen and marker on Kent paper.

マーカーパット●水彩●マーカー

Water color and marker on Marker Pad.

ケント紙●サインペン●スクリーントーン

Felt-tip pen and screen tone on Kent Paper.

ケント紙●サインペン●マーカー●ポスターカラー

Felt-tip pen, marker and poster color on Kent Paper.

ブラウス＆スカート

おしゃれ着として用いるのが多いので，ポーズもおしゃまなきどった雰囲気や，アクセサリーなども小物として演出します。

ケント紙●エボニー鉛筆●水彩

Ebony pencil and water color on Kent paper

Blouses and Skirts

They are often worn dressed up. Choose poses with an elegant and jaunty mood. Accessories to help create the mood.

ケント紙●ボールペン●水彩

Ball-point pen and water color on Kent paper.

画用紙●エボニー鉛筆●水彩

Ebony pencil and water color on paper.

シャツ＆パンツ

全体にカジュアルでラフなスタイルが多いので，ポーズなどもリラックスして
いる雰囲気やタッチを生かして描いてみましょう。

Shirts and Pants

Generally they are more casual and rough in style. Try to produce a relaxed
atmosphere through the choice of appropriate poses.

画用紙●サインペン●マーカー●パステル

Felt-tip pen, marker and pastel on paper.

ケント紙●エボニー鉛筆●マーカー
●水彩●スクリーントーン

*Ebony pencil, marker, water color and
screen tone on Kent paper.*

ケント紙●サインペン●マーカー

Felt-tip pen and marker on Kent paper.

ケント紙●サインペン●マーカー●スクリーントーン

Felt-tip pen, marker and screen tone on Kent paper.

画用紙●エボニー鉛筆●水彩

Ebony pencil and water color on paper.

ワンピース＆ツーピース

カジュアル，ドレッシー，スポーティーといろいろなデザインがありますが，デザインの違いによって，その雰囲気に合ったポーズや帽子・アクセサリー・小物で演出してみましょう。

One-piece and Two-piece Dresses

There are many styles such as casual, dressy and sporty. To produce the best effect for each design, we must choose the right poses, hats and accessories that best fit each design's mood.

ケント紙●サインペン●マーカー

Felt-tip pen and marker on Kent paper.

ケント紙●サインペン●マーカー●ポスターカラー

Felt-tip pen, marker and poster color on Kent paper.

114

ケント紙●エボニー鉛筆●マーカー

Ebony pencil and marker on Kent paper.

ケント紙●エボニー鉛筆●水彩

Ebony pencil and water color on Kent paper.

ナイトウェア

寝るときのためのネグリジェ・パジャマなど，肌に接するものだけに，ボディに馴染む素材感を大切にします。薄手の素材は，ポーズによってボディラインがはっきり出ますが，身体の線ばかりリアルに描くと清潔感を損います。

Nightwear

Negligees and pajamas touch the skin. It is important to express textures that feel good to the touch. The thin materials clearly show the lines of the body in some poses. But the elegance of the designs will be spoiled if you draw the body too realistically.

ケント紙●エボニー鉛筆●グレーインク

Ebony pencil and gray ink on Kent paper.

116

ケント紙●サインペン●スクリーントーン

Felt-tip pen and screen tone on Kent paper.

水着

水着やファンデーションを描く場合は，ボディ（肌）が多く見えるわけですから，
より以上に人体を正確に描けるデッサン力が必要です。
ポーズも動きのある楽しい雰囲気の表現で描きましょう。

Swimwear

In drawing figures in swim suits and foundation garments, a lot of the body is
shown. So the ability to sketch human bodies accurately is more necessary than
usual. Pick out poses rich in movement and give them a cheerful mood.

ケント紙●エボニー鉛筆●パステル

Ebony pencil and pastel on Kent paper.

マーカーパット●サインペン●マーカー
●スクリーントーン

*Felt-tip pen, marker and screen tone
on Marker Pad.*

ケント紙●サインペン●スクリーントーン

Felt-tip pen and screen tone on Kent paper.

コート

コートの素材は，毛皮，ツィード，ニット，ウールなど厚手の生地が多いので，しわなどの描き方も薄手の生地と異ります。またコートの下には洋服を着ていますので，デザインシルエットもたっぷりしています。

Coats

Many materials for coats, shch as fur, tweed and knits, are thick. So the way to draw their folds and wrinkles is different from that used to draw wrinkles in thin clothes. Also clothes are worn under coats, so their design silhouettes are looser.

画用紙●エボニー鉛筆●水彩

Ebony pencil and water color on paper.

画用紙●サインペン●マーカー

Felt-tip pen and marker on paper.

マーカーパット●サインペン●マーカー

Felt-tip pen and marker on Marker Pad.

ニット

ニットの場合，生地と違って全体に身体の線がはっきり出ます。し
わは少なく丸味を出します。ニットの質感を出すためには，線など
もたどたどしいタッチに描くと，より素材感が出ます。

Knits

Knits, unlike cloth, show the line of the body clearly. Draw fewer
wrinkles. Express a round, soft feeling. To capture the feel of knits
well, draw lines with an unsteady touch.

ケント紙●エボニー鉛筆●マーカー

Ebony pencil and marker on Kent paper.

ケント紙●サインペン●マーカー

Felt-tip pen and marker on Kent paper.

画用紙●エボニー鉛筆●水彩

Ebony pencil and water color on paper.

スポーツウェア

楽しく元気で明るく躍動的に描きましょう。健康的なイメージも忘れずに。もちろんデザインに合わせて帽子や小物で演出しましょう。

Sportswear

Draw sportswear cheerful and lively. Remember to create an image of health. Produce various effects by the use of hats and small accessories that complement each design.

ケント紙●エボニー鉛筆●マーカー

Ebony pencil and marker on Kent paper.

マーカーパット●エボニー鉛筆●水彩

Ebony pencil and water color on Marker Pad.

プロフィール

1941年　山形県生まれ。

22歳の時に絵を描きたい一心で上京。デザイン学校でグラフィックの勉強。グラフィックの仕事についたが、自分の本当にやりたい仕事ではないと思い、自分の求めるものを模索している時に、スタイル画教室の広告が目に入り、ファッション イラストレーションを描くきっかけになり、そこで知り合った仲間達と SUN デザイン研究所を設立。1981年退社。

1981年　㈱アトリエ・フロム1を設立

1983年　熊谷小次郎イラスト教室設立

事務所　㈱アトリエ・フロム1

　　　　〒150　東京都渋谷区代官山町20-1

　　　　　　　コムト代官山

　　　　　　　TEL (03)464-6048

PROFILE

Kojiro Kumagai

Born in Yamagata Prefecture, 1941. Came to Tokyo at the age of 22 to have some ambition for art in his mind. Studied graphic design and started as a graphic desiner. However, when he felt something different with it and had asked himself what he should do since then, he happened to know Masao Hara Drawing course. That was his turning point to fashion illustration. After that, he established Sun Design Laboratory with the friends of the Hara course. Resigned there in 1981, established his own office, "Atelier From One".

Head of Atelier From One.

Lectured in Kojiro Kumagai Illustration School.

Atelier From One; Comto Daikanyama, 20-1 Daikanyama-cho, Shibuya-ku, Tokyo 150

Tel. (03)464-6048　Fax (03)464-6052

　　写真撮影　石原　繁徳
　イラスト協力　清水かおる
　　　　　　　吉田　裕子

ファッション イラストレーション
子どもの描き方

1990年12月25日　初版第1刷発行

著　者　熊谷小次郎（くまがいこじろう）©
発行者　久世　利郎

印　刷　錦明印刷株式会社
製　本　大口製本株式会社
写　植　三和写真工芸株式会社

発行所　株式会社グラフィック社
　　　　〒102 東京都千代田区九段北1-9-12
　　　　☎03(263)4318 振替・東京3-114345

翻　訳　ジョセフ・ウオーカー

　　　　浄子・ウオーカー(カラーアナリスト)

ISBN4-7661-0579-6 C3071

モード・ドローイング：顔（男性・女性）
MODE DRAWING : FACE & HEAD(male & female)

矢島 功 著　by Isao Yajima
B4変形判・96頁　size : 268 x 255mm
pages : 96(12 in color)

ファッション ドローイングのテクニック
THE TECHNQUES OF FASHION DRAWING

コリン・バーンズ著　by Colin Barnes
A4変形判・160頁　size : 280 x 213mm
pages : 160(104 in color)

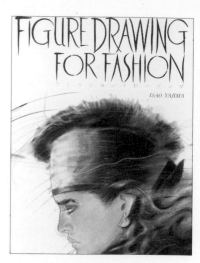

ファッション ドローイング
FIGURE DRAWING FOR FASHION

矢島 功 著　by Isao Yajima
A4変形判・128頁　size : 300 x 225mm
pages : 128 (96 in color)

モード・ドローイング：ヌード（女性）
MODE DRAWING : NUDE(female)

矢島 功 著　by Isao Yajima
B4変形判・110頁　size : 268 x 255mm
pages : 110(2 in color)

モード・ドローイング：ヌード（男性）
MODE DRAWING : NUDE(male)

矢島 功 著　by Isao Yajima
B4変形判・108頁　size : 268 x 255mm
pages : 108

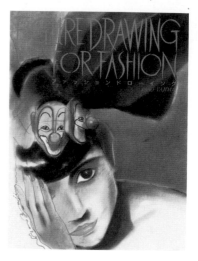

ファッション ドローイング②
FIGURE DRAWING FOR FASHION 2

矢島 功 著　by Isao Yajima
A4変形判・128頁　size : 300 x 225mm
pages : 128 (96 in color)

モード・ドローイング：コスチューム（女性）
MODE DRAWING : COSTUME(female)

矢島 功 著　by Isao Yajima
B4変形判・84頁　size : 268 x 255mm
pages : 84(24 in color)

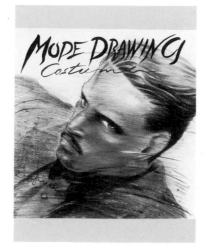

モード・ドローイング：コスチューム（男性）
MODE DRAWING : COSTUME(male)

矢島 功 著　by Isao Yajima
B4変形判・84頁　size : 268 x 255mm
pages : 84(24 in color)

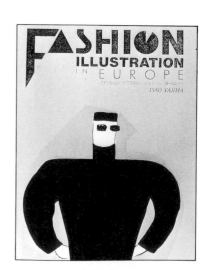

ファッション イラストレーション イン ヨーロッパ
FASHION ILLUSTRATION IN EUROPE

矢島 功 編　by Isao Yajima
A4変形判・126頁　size : 300 x 225mm
pages : 126 (110 in color)